STEAM'S LAMENT

London Midland Engine Sheds
Volume II - 8A to 12E

Kevin Derrick

Strathwood

STEAM'S LAMENT

London Midland Engine Sheds
Volume II - 8A to 12E

First published 2019
ISBN 978-1-905276-97-4

Copyright Strathwood Publishing 2019
Published by Strathwood Publishing, 9 Boswell Crescent, Inverness, IV2 3ET
Telephone 01463 234004
Printed by Akcent Media, Ltd.
www.strathwood.co.uk

Contents

This volume is compiled on the basis of the shed codes of 1948-1950 wherever possible

Opposite: A relaxed moment outside the sheds at Liverpool's 8A Edge Hill around 1961, as there is a chance for a chat from the footplate of 14D Neasden's Britannia 70045 Lord Rowallan with a couple of lads before they are due off shed, meanwhile alongside the safety valves begin to lift onboard 46240 City of Coventry. *Late Jim Carter/Rail Online*

In March 1961, 46229 Duchess of Hamilton was transferred from 5A Crewe North to here at 8A Edge Hill, this would be the locomotive's last transfer until withdrawal in February 1964. Certainly, in this view one of Stanier's masterpieces, as she makes her way off shed tender first, there were no thoughts of a gleaming preserved locomotive. *Colour Rail*

Opposite: In the spring of 1962, Royal Scot 46167 The Hertfordshire Regiment displays an 8F Wigan Springs Branch shed code as she basks in the sunshine outside the once huge engine sheds here in the ex-LNWR territory at Edge Hill. *Late Jim Carter/Rail Online*

In this pleasing elevated view of 46229 Duchess of Hamilton, she appears to be in more respectable condition complete with a tender full of what looks to be good quality coal for her next top link duty away from Edge Hill around 1962. *Late Jim Carter/Rail Online*

The distinctive overhead coaling plant here at Edge Hill was built in 1914 during the shed's LNWR days and remained in use until closure to steam in 1968, soon after this scene was recorded. *Strathwood Library Collection*

Another view of the Edge Hill coaling plant from another direction as Jubilee 45741 Leinster from 12B Carlisle Upperby has just taken a refill of coal around 1961.
Late Jim Carter/Rail Online

Although Edge Hill engine shed enjoyed a heritage from the London & North Western Railway and an abundance of that company's locomotives up until the end of the Second World War. The LMS had already begun to replace the older ex-LNWR types with designs from the ex-Lancashire & Yorkshire Railway in the area such as this 1878 built Aspinall Class 23 0-6-0ST, which in turn would give way to withdrawal in 1957. *Strathwood Library Collection*

As the first Chief Mechanical Engineer for the LMS in 1923 Hughes began the design of this mogul, which would be brought to fruition under the reign of Fowler as the holder of this post from 1926. This example was built during 1930 and spent the first twelve years of its British Railway's career allocated to 9A Longsight meaning it was no stranger on shed here at Edge Hill. *Strathwood Library Collection*

This former Lancashire & Yorkshire Railway built Class 27 designed by Aspinall was transferred here to 8A and renumbered from its former LMS number 12118 in August 1948 from Warrington's Dallam shed. At this time around early 1949 there were three others in her class also allocated here to Edge Hill. This example would move away to Springs Branch during 1952 and in 1954 head to the cutting yard most likely within Horwich Works after being stripped of anything useful. *The Transport Treasury*

Opposite: With their fires dropped around 1959, both Patriot 45539 E.C. Trench and Royal Scot 46155 The Lancer have been stopped to be worked upon by the Edge Hill fitters on their home shed and will hopefully be back in service again very soon. *Late Jim Carter/Rail Online*

Another large ex-LNWR engine shed was situated at Warrington Dallam coded 8B through until closure on 2 October 1967. The nine-road engine shed was re-roofed by British Railways during 1957 and is seen here on 15 May 1966 with a track gang renewing a sleeper in the shed yard. *Rail Online*

Opposite: We can see that the new roof complete with full-length smoke cowls has made the working conditions for the fitting staff reasonably comfortable to begin work on Patriot 45549 within its home shed on 3 September 1961. *David T.Williams*

The condition of 12B Carlisle Upperby's Black Five 45397 reflects a recent works visit in this shot from 1961 as an Ivatt Class 2MT blocks its route away from the turntable at Warrington Dallam. *Rail Online*

Opposite: The London Midland Region liked to remind it's staff of the rebuilding year when it re-invested in its infrastructure as here on the new roof at Dallam. Outside the shed during the following year is one of 8B's own Aspinall Class 27s, complete with a double sprung tender. *Rail Online*

Taken from the footplate of a passing goods train during July 1965, things do not look so good for this duo of freshly withdrawn Class 4F 0-6-0s, 44115 and 44349 along with an unknown Jubilee, all dumped alongside the shed here at Warrington Dallam. *Late Jim Carter/Rail Online*

The best days for Dallam shed are very much behind us in this view from the road bridge overlooking the shed yard on 11 June 1966, with less than four months until closure. Aside from the BMC 1100 in the yard's car park one of the short-lived Hunslet diesel shunters D2562 mingles with Class 8F, 48612 and Black five 45055. *Rail Online*

Opposite: There is just one bicycle in the rack located within Dallam's airy shed roof on 15 May 1966 as all is quiet on a Sunday. There was still a variety to the motive power to be seen hereabouts that early summer. The shed's allocation had fallen from almost sixty locomotives just after nationalization to around thirty by this stage. *Rail Online*

A number of the rebuilt former Crosti-boiler Class 9Fs were allocated to both 8C Speke Junction and to 8H Birkenhead during the mid-sixties. This example spent time at both sheds during this period and as such would not have been a stranger here at 8B Warrington Dallam in 1966.
Keith Langston/Rail Photoprints

A small sub-shed to Warrington Dallam was located at Warrington Arpley, this arose from the opening of the line from Warrington to Timperley which was constructed by The Warrington and Altrincham Junction Railway in 1854, this was later absorbed within the LNWR and after the grouping into the LMS. Remarkably perhaps this engine shed remained in use in spite of its close proximity to its parent shed at Dallam until 27 May 1963. The location was then used as a diesel stabling and signing on point for long after Dallam had closed. The upper view dates from 1958 with Class 8F 48424 in residence with something else lurking within the shadows inside the shed. Our lower view was taken on 19 April 1953 of the rear of the shed building with the sand house to the right-hand side of Dallam's Class 3F 43237, the ex-L&Y Aspinall Class 2P 50644 was a new arrival to the area just a few weeks beforehand from 10B Preston previously.
Both: Strathwood Library Collection

Left: The shed at Speke Junction later coded as 8C in both LMS and British Railway's days came about as a means to reduce light engine movements from Edge Hill to the sidings at Speke for the LNWR. On 16 May 1967, it was providing sanctuary to Class 9F 92046 from Birkenhead. *Derek Jones*

Below: A wider panorama from 1962 reveals how the shed's allocation of diesel shunters was segregated in the four roads to the right in this view.
Strathwood Library Collection

Although 8C Speke Junction saw a number of improvements during the fifties, the old coal hole with its water tank above was retained being joined by new mechanical coal and ash plants. Several fellow enthusiasts bunk around the shed during early 1967 witnessing another of the now exiled rebuilt ex-Crosti Class 9Fs simmering nicely in the winter sunshine. *Rail Online*

The ash tubs are full and piles of the spent by-product lay all around the 1950s built ash plant here at Speke on 1 May 1967, with a Stanier Class 8F 48704 alongside one of the Caprotti Black Fives 44753.
Win Wall/Strathwood Library Collection

This all contrasts with the ash shovel lain against the cab of this Aspinall Class 2F on shed here at Speke Junction on 11 September 1954.
Strathwood Library Collection

The black smoke suggests the fireman on-board this Class 9F is making up his fire ready for the road once again at Speke Junction on 18 February 1967. *Colour Rail*

The LNWR located another shed at Widnes in the junction of the Liverpool to Manchester and St.Helens route with a line that gave access to Widnes Docks. Coded as 8D in the British Railway's era it was home to almost thirty locomotives. It had previously been a sub-shed to Brunswick who maintained the locomotives that often used the ex-Cheshire Lines Committee shed at Widnes Tanhouse Lane just a mile away from the shed here at Widnes where Austerity 2-8-0 90242 was on shed in 1961. *Rail Online*

Another 1961 view of the east end of 8D Widnes shed looking north from the long footbridge, the shed's turntable at the east of the shed is below the viaduct of the Liverpool to Manchester route, the Liverpool to St. Helens lines run between the Stanier Class 8F acting as shed pilot in the background and the two withdrawn Stanier Class 3MTs dumped in the sidings in the foreground. Note the crude scaffolding electrification training set up for footplate staff, the shed closed on 13 April 1964. *Rail Online*

An elevated 1953 view of the former Cheshire Lines Committee shed at Brunswick coded variously as 13E in 1949, then as 8E from 1950 until 1958 when it became 27F until it was closed on 11 September 1961. In the background is Herculaneum station on the Liverpool Overhead Railway which closed in 1956. The Depot was situated in an extraordinarily cramped site beside the CLC line from Liverpool Central, which here came out briefly from the sequence of smoky tunnels that led into the terminus, to serve also the large Brunswick Goods Station.
Strathwood Library Collection

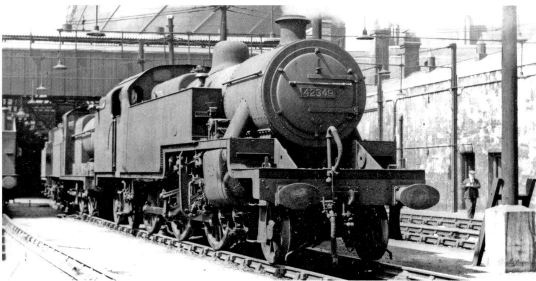

The ex-CLC sheds such as Brunswick employed mainly ex-LNER locomotives before nationalisation, then as part of the London Midland Region, more ex-LMS types arrived too. Here, ex-GC Class D9 4-4-0 62318 is seen on 2 September 1949 just two months before it was withdrawn. Another visit in late 1958 finds Fowler Class 4MT 42349 standing in the remains of what was its then home shed here at Brunswick as 27F.
Photos: Rail Photoprints & Strathwood Library Collection

Similarly, in May 1949 it was the impressive appearance of another ex-GCR locomotive in the shape of Robinson Class D10 62658 Prince George that caught our cameraman's eye. The shed's turntable was tucked in below the rock cutting with Grafton Street directly above this high sided tender fitted Class 4F 44587, which was being turned on 12 November 1960.
Both: Strathwood Library Collection

The parlous state of 9A Longsight's 'old' or 'south' shed roof is clear on 24 August 1955 with Fowler Class 4MT 42367 enjoying a boiler washout while it was allocated to 5D Stoke at the time. *Rail Online*

Another view of the 'old' or 'south' shed the following year highlights just how dirty and sooty engine sheds could be with another Fowler Class 4MT to the fore. *Rail Photoprints*

Opposite: Inside at Longsight, fitters have been working on this ex-LNWR Class G2A 49093 in from 1E Bletchley after it had been stopped alongside a Fowler Class 4F on 22 February 1962. *Strathwood Library Collection*

With the carriage shed in the background Longsight's Jubilee 45671 Prince Rupert is on its home shed during 1959. *Rail Photoprints*

As part of the 1959 rebuilding works modifications were made towards converting Longsight shed to accommodate the new diesels and overhead AC electric locomotives, although at this time the latter was being kept away from the former steam shed. Throughout the fifties, Longsight's allocation of steam locomotives shrunk from around one hundred and thirty at the start of the British Railway's era to final elimination on 14 February 1965. On a bright and sunny 22 February 1962, Fairburn Class 4MT 42137 was still to be found here alongside one of the fueling bowsers for the new diesels, this 9A allocated tank engine would shortly be re-allocated to 5F Uttoxeter. *Rail Online*

Opposite: By 3 September 1961, the overhead gantries were very much a prominent feature at Longsight as this Fowler Class 4MT from 9B Stockport Edgeley acts as the yard and carriage shed pilot for the day.
David T. Williams

Several withdrawn locomotives remained stored here at Longsight for a few years awaiting their last journey to the breakers. One such example was Stanier Class 3MT 40084 which was withdrawn in November 1959 until heading to the Central Wagon Co. at Ince near Wigan in May 1961.
Strathwood Library Collection

Opposite: Another appearance for Fowler Class 4MT 42316, this time on its home shed here at 9B Stockport Edgeley on 29 June 1961, where again it finds itself on shed pilot duties for the day. *Colour Rail*

Once again, the recent arrival of the electrification gantries here alongside the shed at Stockport Edgeley catches our eyes as this Hughes/Fowler Crab makes its way off the shed on 8 April 1961. *Colour Rail*

Just a year previously the mainline seen in the background was still signalled by semaphores as the gangers attend to their duties within the shed yard alongside the 'coal hole' and Austerity 90078 visiting Stockport from Hull Dairycoates. Another eight coupled visitor to the shed on 7 June 1960 was 9D Buxton's Class G2 49281. *Both: Colour Rail*

A view looking southwards of the shed here at Stockport Edgeley on 9 September 1967 with Black Five 45261 being prepared for duty. Originally a north-light style of roof covered the shed here which was renewed by the LMS in the early thirties. *Jerry Beddows*

Opposite; The next numerical Black Five 45262 is recorded here too around 1964 alongside a Sulzer Type2 as the Stanier 4-6-0 awaits the coal elevator to be put to good use to top up its tender. *Rail Online*

A second view here during 1967 shows that with a reduced steam allocation at Stockport Edgeley the queue for the coal elevator has eased considerably and there is time for conversation with a group of young spotters as they watch Class 8F 48546 about to be topped up with coal once more. *Strathwood Library Collection*

Some beefy chunks of coal adorn the tender of another of Stanier's Class 8Fs, as the fireman of 48437 attends to his water supply before heading off shed for the locomotive's next freight turn from the ex-LNWR built water tank above the original coaling facilities. *Strathwood Library Collection*

Opposite: Two of the 9B shed staff are happy to stop for a moment their duties clearing spent ash to allow Black Five 44781 to roll past with her cylinder drain-cocks open on 20 April 1968. Notice the track's sleepers at this point are protected from being burnt by hot discarded ashes.
Keith Widdowson/Anistr.com

On the morning of 29 October 1966, Ivatt Class 2MT 41204 has been smartened up to work today's R.C.T.S. organized Stoke-on-Trent area brake van tour. Final preparations are being made before heading away from Stockport Edgeley shed to start this special duty.
Strathwood Library Collection

Left: The small two-road ex-LNWR shed at Macclesfield 9C had been a sub-shed to 39A Gorton from 1950 until 1958 when it assumed the vacant code of 9C. We see it on 19 June 1960 with a couple of Fowler Class 4MTs on shed, closure came on 11 June the following year. *Gerald T. Robinson*

Below: The ex-LNWR shed at Buxton still retained much of its original Webb style of roof when recorded in May 1956. Coded 9D until 9 September 1963, when the far larger shed at Newton Heath took over this code, reducing Buxton down the ranks to be coded as 9L until closure to steam on 2 March 1968. *Colour Rail*

Fellow spotters roam free-range around 9D Buxton as part of an organized society visit during 1963. The shed's allocation had fallen from over fifty locomotives at the start of the fifties to less than thirty by this point, mainly due to the use of DMUs on the shed's former passenger turns.
Strathwood Library Collection

This page & opposite: Another society visit to 9D Buxton during 1963 was made on 11 May when the R.C.T.S. and the Locomotive Club of Great Britain jointly organized the North Midlands Railtour. This started from St. Pancras behind Bulleid Pacific 34006 Bude just before 9 am. Things did not go so well behind Bude, leaving 4 minutes late, the tour lost time all the way, leaving the Bedford stop 48 minutes down, by the time Derby was reached this was now 80 minutes behind time, therefore tour participants did not visit the works as had been originally arranged. At Derby, this Class B1 was put on, as a result, things improved but the turnaround here at Buxton was reduced by twenty-six minutes, hence spotters would have to be fleet of foot to get around Buxton shed as they attempted to get back on time. Both views show how Buxton shed was situated on an exposed site on elevated moorland often subject to dreadful weather conditions.

Photos: Rail Photoprints & Strathwood Library Collection

By 1966, it was not unusual to find locomotives off the Cromford & High Peak such as this Class J94 68006. The roof had gone by this time and any investment by British Railways in the town was only being allocated to the new diesel facilities adjacent to the station.

Photos: Strathwood Library Collection & Rail Online

Thirty years beforehand the LMS had invested in this coal plant being visited by another Class J94 dressed, with extra weather protection during 1966.
Strathwood Library Collection

68012

Top: The former Cheshire Lines Committee shed at Trafford Park was coded as 19F at nationalization, this soon changed to 13A, then to 9E all before 22 May 1950. Settling down as 9E until 1956, then to 17F from January 1957 until 20 April 1958, only to revert back to 9E up to closure on 2 March 1968.

Bottom: Two of the Parker/Pollitt Class N5s are seen here at the now roofless Trafford Park shed on 16 June 1951 and 22 April of the same year respectively.
Both: Strathwood Library Collection

Opposite: A further call in here the same year found one of Derby's Class 4P compounds outside what remained of this extensive twenty-road shed.
Rail Photoprints

The end will soon arrive for the Robinson Class D9 62305 seen within Trafford Park's shed yard during March 1950, it was withdrawn four months later. Likewise a further clear out of ex-Great Central Railway locomotives would see this Class J10 and N5 marked up for scrapping here too 3 October 1954.
Strathwood Library Collection

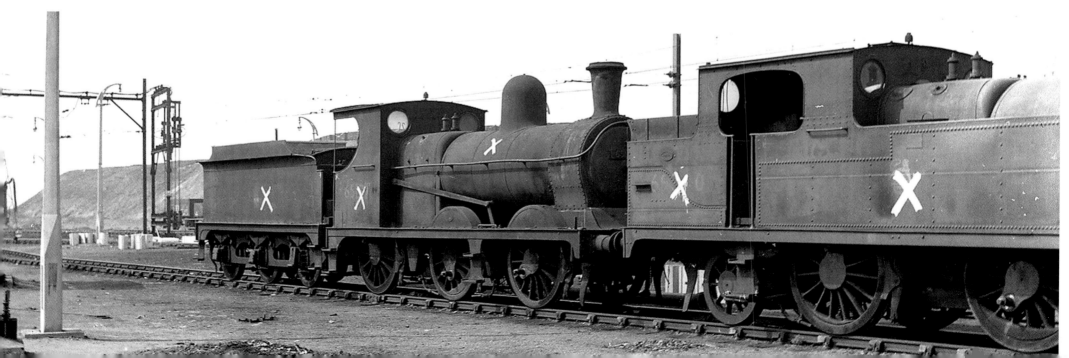

Although the bent running plate of 62661 Gerard Powys Dewhurst is damaged in this 1953 view within Trafford Park's extensive shed yard, this ex-GCR Class D11 would remain in traffic until November of 1960. *Rail Photoprints*

Using the wonder material of the age, some repairs were made to the roof structures that survived here at Trafford Park 15 October 1967 when both Black Five 44665 and Class 8F 48763 were photographed on shed here. *Both: Gerald T. Robinson*

Another view of the run-down steam scene in the area with an absence of shed plates and roof structure here at 9F Heaton Mersey shed with another Black five and Class 8F line-up as a recent starter to the railway sets about clearing the smokebox of ash from one of the Class 8Fs in 1968.
Strathwood Library Collection

A visit to record the shed's final activities found Class 8F 48356 along with several others out of steam here on 4 May 1968, the day before closure. *Jerry Beddows*

Opposite: Preservation thanks to the artist David Shepherd would save this Class 9F 92203 stabled outside at Heaton Mersey on 20 August 1967, but alas although a new diesel servicing shed was constructed nearby here during 1965, both sheds would close officially on 5 May 1968. *Late Jim Carter/Rail Photoprints*

The coal man looks down from his lofty position in the coal stage onto the cab this ex-Crosti Class 9F, as 92027 completes coaling at Heaton Mersey on 7 May 1966. *Colour Rail*

Opposite: Standard Class 9F 92054 stands alongside Stanier Class 5MT Mogul 42947 the year beforehand on 8 August at Heaton Mersey on the outskirts of Stockport. *Bill Wright*

67

Bolton was served by two sheds, the smaller one was the ex-LNWR establishment here at Plodder Lane, whereas the far larger shed in the town was originally for the Lancashire & Yorkshire Railway. Coded 10D within the London Midland Region with only a small allocation it was an early closure in October 1954, as a result, it was seldom photographed. This push & pull fitted Ivatt Class 2MT was new from Crewe Works in September 1948 joining the stable of locomotives here that October it was sent away to Chester after five years in September 1953. *Rail Online*

Opposite: Sutton Oak shed near St. Helens also enjoyed an ex-LNWR lineage passing into British Railways as 10E with a nine-road engine shed it carried an allocation of almost forty locomotives. As both the two nearest stations Sutton Oak and Peasley Cross were closed visits using public transport meant either a bus from St. Helens or a forty-minute walk, as a result, it was another shed less covered by cameramen of the day. A year after the closure of 10D Plodder Lane, it was decided that Sutton Oak should become the new 10D. This view here at the new 10D Sutton Oak shows home allocated Class G2 49288 having its ashpan cleaned out on 2 June 1957. *Cecil Sanderson/The Transport Treasury*

Also alongside the 'coal hole' which was still in use as there was no large mechanical coaler installed here at Sutton Oak was another Class G2 49377 still showing the 10E shed code in 1955. *Strathwood Library Collection*

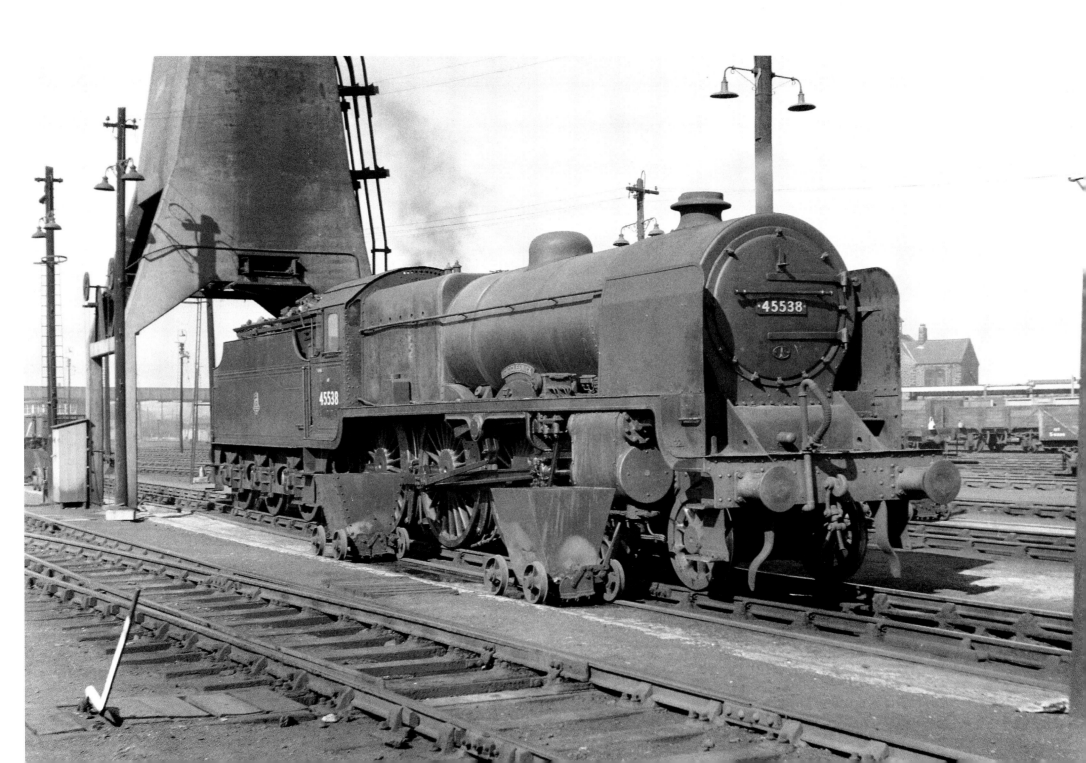

There was still two years of service ahead for this filthy Caprotti fitted Standard Class 5MT when it was seen sleeping quietly in Carnforth shed's northern sidings on 30 April 1966.
Win Wall/Strathwood Library Collection

Another 4-6-0 showing signs of recent priming in these sidings at Carnforth on 6 August 1967, was one of Kingmoor's Black Fives 44817. *Gerald T. Robinson*

Opposite: Looking northwards from the access footbridge to the shed yard here at Carnforth on 29 April 1967, provides a view towards the far end of the shed yard past several stored Black Fives including the now preserved 45025 along with 44894 which would not be scrapped until May 1969 at the hands of Drapers in Hull. Carnforth's shed codes changed through the years from 11A until 1958, then as 24L before becoming 10A from 1963 until closure on 5 August 1968. *Jerry Beddows*

A similar view from 30 April the year previously shows spotters roaming free range all around the shed yard here at Carnforth. They had arrived onboard the Jubilee Railway Society's South Yorkshireman No.5 Railtour. This tour was originally advertised for haulage by 45565 Victoria throughout however the loco was not available, so 45593 Kolhapur seen here was substituted. Unfortunately, this Jubilee too was also later failed at Carlisle with Britannia 70035 Rudyard Kipling taking over. The tour's participants still managed visits not only to Carnforth but also to both Carlisle's Kingmoor and Upperby sheds too.

Win Wall/Strathwood Library Collection

New diesels are beginning to mingle among the majority which was still very much steam at Carnforth by July 1965, with a healthy reserve of coal awaiting emptying into the mechanical coal plant.
Strathwood Library Collection

Opposite: Another scene by the mechanical ash plant at Carnforth eight years after our previous view shows the changes to the regular motive power which were becoming less glamorous by 7 October 1967.
Late Norman Preedy/Rail Photoprints

Both the ash and coal plants at Carnforth can be seen as Class 8F 48384 and an unknown Class 9F mingle in the lines for servicing during March 1967.
Peter Simmonds

Perhaps there are some concerns about the track below Black Five 45342 or maybe with the water crane that accounts for this gathering at Carnforth on 3 September 1967?
Gerald T. Robinson

Opposite: Withdrawn Standard Class 9Fs await their ultimate fate in the lines at Carnforth, some still have full tenders, perhaps they were to have been steamed to the scrapyards as the embers were dying fast all across the north-west by 14 June 1968. *Rail Online*

Likewise, the view from the access footbridge reveals a mix of Black Fives, Class 8Fs and a solitary 9F also held in limbo as they await purchases for scrap and on how they will make their last journeys too in early 1968.
Strathwood Library Collection

Unlike Carnforth, the former Furness Railway shed at Barrow was to have been less the subject for visitors and cameramen alike in the age of steam. At the start of the British Railway's era, it was coded as 11B with an allocation of some fifty locomotives. On 20 April 1958, Barrow assumed the former shed code of Carnforth becoming the new 11A. This would change once more three years later as it became 12E. The shed also became one of the homes for the hapless Metropolitan Vickers Co-Bos during the sixties. Then the code changed once again to 12C in 1963. Steam ceased here at Barrow on 12 December 1966 although diesels continued to use the shed until 1977 long after both steam and the dreaded Co-Bos had gone. *Rail Online*

Left: Another of Gresley's A3s was to be found here at Carlisle Canal on 14 August 1956, in the shape of 60041 Salmon Trout from 64B Edinburgh Haymarket. *Strathwood Library Collection*

Opposite: The ex-LNWR shed at Penrith had been the original 12C until 8 October 1955 when it was given the code of 12B and then made as an un-coded sub-shed to Upperby from 1958. It would close completely along with Oxenholme on 18 June 1962. The appearance of Ivatt Class 2MT 46449 which was new in 1950 suggests this view was taken at Penrith soon afterwards. *Rail Online*

Right: A link back to the days of the North British Railway next on 15 July 1950, with the last one of the Holmes Class D31s 62281 to be allocated here at Canal, it was withdrawn in December 1952. *Strathwood Library Collection*

A real relic from the former London & North Western Railway was to be found lurking inside the small two-road shed at Penrith in the early fifties. This Webb designed 'Cauliflower' 0-6-0 is not only one of the very last survivors of her class but is also fitted with a tender coal cover to keep snow out when used on the exposed routes in the area, it was withdrawn in December 1955. *Strathwood Library Collection*

Above: The changes and improvements to 12D Workington repairing the damaged roof structure along with new mechanical coaling facilities took place soon after this first view from 1954.
Ben Brooksbank Collection

Right: These rebuilding works also coincided with the early introduction of DMUs into the Workington area which meant that five of the roads on the west side of the shed on the left here in this 1965 view were reserved for diesels only.
Strathwood Library Collection

The segregation between the then-new Derby Lightweight DMUs and the slightly older Ivatt Class 2MT Moguls is clearly evident in this scene taken on 14 April 1957. When 46447 arrived here at Workington in May 1950 the shed code was still 12D, it would become 12C from 1955 until 1958, then 11B up to 1960. Next, it was given 12F taking us as far as 1963 before reverting back to its original code of 12D to take it through to closure with steam as of 1 January 1968. The shed buildings were then used to house DMUs and diesel locomotives for a while afterwards.
Rail Online

An early fifties view of another of 12D Workington's Ivatt Class 2MT Moguls acting as the shed pilot lending a shove to one of the surviving Pettigrew designed ex-Furness Railway Class 3F 0-6-0s. *Rail Online*

Originally the former ex-LNWR/Furness Railway's shed at Moor Row had been a much busier four-road shed with a substantial stone frontage. However, post-war it had become very rundown with the possibility of either complete closure or some form of budget rebuilding being required. Inevitably perhaps British Railways adopted the latter path, by cutting the shed back to just two roads with a fresh timber roof going up. Inside on 7 May 1954, one of the ex-Furness Railway Class 3Fs complete with the original style of boiler is being prepared for the lunchtime Millom goods. The view from outside on 25 March 1950 reveals a Class 2P, Jinty and an ex-L&YR Aspinall Class 27 with at least three more engines hiding inside the shed coded 12E until closure on 31 July 1954.

Both: Strathwood Library Collection